Contents

List of Tables

1
Introduction

Background

In 2005, the average chief executive officer (CEO) of the top 1,000 largest public-ranked companies by sales earned $9.025 billion. The monetary value stood just below the gross domestic product (GDP) of Jamaica, whose GDP was $9.71 billion (Walsh, 2008). Presently, CEO compensation is being scrutinized in terms of short-term versus long-term consequences relative to organizational performance. There has been a new emphasis on restructuring compensation agreements, changing CEO's incentives, and providing succession planning in organizations (Coster, 2010). Beginning in 1992, the Securities and Exchange Commission (SEC) required a more refined level of information regarding CEO compensation, which was segmented into salary, bonus, options, stock, and long-standing incentives (Hurt, 2003).

According to Bryan, Hwang, and Lilien (2000), there was an immediate reaction to the tremendous increase in the stock-based portion of CEO compensation, and the SEC required organizations to provide much greater detail of the compensation factors in their proxy statements. The requirements included, but were not confined to, knowledge of salary, bonuses, stock options, restricted stock, and long-term incentives. As a result, CEO compensation appears to be moving toward a greater emphasis on longer term incentives, performance-based rewards, and increased alignment with shareholder interests (Coster, 2010).

The United States is now facing a new precedent in regulating CEO compensation with the CEOs being pressured to appease governmental regulators and, as a result of this development, the financial sector will no doubt become the center of attention. Formerly, the Sarbanes-Oxley Act of 2002 affected the CEO compensation debate in a powerful fashion and, combined with the current public demand for greater accountability, there is an even greater challenge to the dialogue surrounding this issue (Coster, 2010).

The Sarbanes-Oxley Act of 2002 had two main components. The first was

Section 302, which pertained to senior management certifying the correctness and precision of the organizational financial statement, and the second, Section 404, requiring public companies' management to report and maintain detailed internal controls. The second section has been expensive for the public companies due to the cost of tracking the internal controls (Kuschnik, 2008).

Many of the CEOs' increased salaries have been the result of comparison and competition among fellow CEOs. The results have come in the form of CEOs contending to increase their salary weighed against a competitor's earnings. According to Warren Buffet, CEO compensation will continue to climb unless it is more closely tied to organizational performance rather than to organizational peer group's salaries (Bogle, 2008).

There has been a movement to avoid compensation packages that allow the CEOs to engage in precarious decision making motivated by bonuses that are greatly connected with revenue generation deadlines. Executive board members are also facing heightened pressure as the shareholders expect a greater sense of corporate responsibility. In turn, this leads to top executives making an effort to become more involved with the CEOs' responsibilities in requiring the CEOs to handle and address the concerns of executive members to a finer degree.

In October 2009, Legal Bulletin No. 14E of the Securities and Exchange Commission (SEC) encouraged corporations to create and implement CEO succession planning strategies. In the face of this controversy, succession planning is currently moving to the forefront of many corporations and is one of their primary concerns, as their CEOs are being faced with the occasionally unruly task of planning for their own future departure. In the past, many CEOs completely ignored succession planning for their organizations and, as a result, these institutions are beginning to understand and realize that hiring a competent CEO is a more difficult process than it ever has been in the past (Coster, 2010).

The researcher's experience in this area is a combination of both academic review and first-hand knowledge and involvement with CEO practices from individual working relationships. In reviewing these compensation issues, which are related specifically to a CEO, the researcher has often been fascinated with the differing opinions that appear to exist among the general public regarding this issue, particularly after having a variety of personal experiences in different types of industries where there have been struggles with the issue of CEO compensation, notably in both the financial and insurance industries. It has generally been felt that there have been numerous instances where some CEOs have been overpaid while others have demonstrated that they have definitely generated their worth. This subject has often created a polarizing debate and, when it is addressed in social settings, it usually ends in strong disagreement from both sides.

The researcher has noticed that even relatively moderate opinions on the subject have provoked feelings of frustration from those who disagree and believe that the system is heavily weighted in favor of the CEOs. Although there are many people who are in agreement, there is a need to understand that, as a society, some responsibility should also be taken for examining a system that has been allowed to go relatively unchecked and monitored in the past.

Building on this point, Latham (2007) addressed this subject through the term *psychological contract,* which can be defined as perceived fairness between two parties that have been dishonored by one or both of the parties. It is considered to be an unwritten set of guidelines that are to be followed by all parties. An example of this is the distinctive thought process that exists between employees and their employers, especially when one concludes that another has received an unfair benefit. Additionally, Coyle-Shapiro and Conway (2005) noted that

> In relationships characterized by increasing levels of organizational support, the importance of a psychological contract in terms of felt obligations recedes into the background, whereas in relationships characterized by decreasing organizational support, employees are more likely to invoke the psychological contract, possibly as a means of regulating a deteriorating relationship. (p. 237)

The importance of these findings was that the key point to creating incentives for positive participative behavior in group members is not just completion of the psychological contract, but rather what the workers receive and what they think they will receive in the future (Coyle-Shapiro & Conway, 2005). These concepts articulate the essence of the lack of perceived fairness that has come to the attention of the public on the subject of CEO compensation and its relationship to organizational performance.

Organizational justice has become a core notion not only between the employee and his or her employer, but rather among the general public. It refers to a system that is composed of distinctive divisions that contribute to the whole, which exists in relationship to the components of a CEO's compensation package. Thus, this project chose to observe some of those components associated with firm performance and executive reimbursement. It appears that there is a lack of detailed knowledge on the nuances of the CEO compensation structure, and it has just recently moved to the forefront where there has been some interest and focus directed to this issue, which is finally receiving some well-deserved attention in the media and from the public. The perspectives on the subject of compensation are vast and encompass many different areas of study. Organizational development by design includes many of these factors and issues, noting that each one needs to be individually considered when strategizing and addressing the future of CEO compensation.

Purpose

The purpose of this research project was to understand and explore the relationship of the chief executive officers' (CEOs') compensation to organizational performance in multinational, public insurance organizations. The major focus was to address the reimbursement component of the total compensation package of the chief executive officers within *Forbes Magazine's Global 2000* listing of the top 20 insurance companies in the United States of America (USA) in 2009, evaluating their organizational performances for 3 previous years (2007-2009) and understanding any possible relationships between the two.

Shen, Gentry, and Tosi (2010) noted that CEO executive compensation has been at previously unheard of levels of scrutiny and unparalleled heights of attention from shareholders. There has been a consequence to the perceived disproportional CEO compensation as compared to employees' salaries in organizations and other executives that are closely aligned with CEOs. The examination of CEO reimbursement has intensified with the CEOs' compensation exceeding six times the earnings of the compensation of their closest colleagues. Because of these events, an assessment of CEO reimbursement has become an important issue in business negotiations in many organizations.

The research question was divided into three different subhypotheses regarding related compensation factors and the relationship to organizational performance, to determine if any of the following existed: (a) Hypothesis 1--There is a significant relationship between CEO total compensation and firm performance, (b) Hypothesis 2--There is a significant relationship between CEO base salary and company performance, and (c) Hypothesis 3--There is a significant relationship between previous year's organizational performance and CEO compensation.

These factors included comparing global insurance companies, rank, CEO types of compensation, and incentive packages. The top 20 *Forbes Magazine's Global 2000* insurance firms in 2009 were evaluated for their organizational performance relative to the industry averages in their perspective categories.

The research methodology for this project utilized a test-research design, focusing on the use of both archival and public data and examining total compensation for CEOs and related organizational performance in association with other comparable organizations. The data were extracted from the public sources of Forbes.com, SEC filings from 10-ks and 14As statements, proxy statements, and focused on the pretax return of equity (pretax ROE), earnings per share (EPS), debt-to-equity, revenue, and the organizational performances for the years of 2009, 2008, and 2007.

This study includes five chapters. Chapter 2 follows, which is a review of the related literature, presenting a background and history of chief executive compensation, benefits, and associated challenges of implementing a chief executive officer compensation program and the possible ways in which to connect it to organizational performance within the insurance industry. The chapter examines the best practices that have been utilized for evaluating CEO compensation strategies and how they are being measured in various organizations. Chapter 3, Methodology, describes how the archival and public data were analyzed to determine CEO compensation in relation to organizational performance, and a summary is provided for organizational performance that is compared to CEO compensation in the top 20 *Forbes Magazine's 200* public insurance companies for the year 2009 and includes data related back to the year 2007. Chapter 4 presents the results, which include a synopsis of the analysis of the data and the findings that emerged. Chapter 5 offers a discussion of proposals for future research of CEO compensation and organizational performance, as well as summarizing the strengths and weaknesses of current compensation practices. It also presents the current issues that are related to CEO compensation and offers suggestions for exploration into new areas of this subject matter.

2
Literature Review

Background

The literature specifically focuses on chief executive officer (CEO) compensation and the relationship to organization performance in public, multinational insurance companies in the United States of America (USA). The theories and powerful influences that have been associated with the growth and maturation of aligning CEO compensation comparatively to the organizational performance outcomes are presented and reviewed.

Boumosleh, Cline, and Saleh (2009) found that the CEOs were facing revolutionary situations in the face of mounting pressure for producing extraordinary results. In effect, their roles have become more vital than ever to securing valued organizational performance outcomes. The importance of the issue has also been reinforced by the many legislative bills, enacted legislation, and laws, ranging from The Reconciliation Act of 1993 to the Sarbanes-Oxley Act of 2002. Enactments such as these regulations have been proposed, highly debated, and ratified during the last 25 years in numerous governmental agencies.

History of CEO Compensation

The apparent inequities of the CEO payment and reward system have created a public outcry for continued debates and adjustments to the negotiated CEO compensation packages. Further exacerbating this situation is the perception that apparent and unwarranted bonuses have recently reached an all-time high for those CEOs who have been granted them.

Lo (2006) noted that executives are hired to control tremendous amounts of equity that affect their organizations. The examination of the relationship between firm performance variables related to the compensation components that are received are an important issue to the shareholders. Specifically, scrutiny has been focused on the surplus salaries of CEOs when compared to their actualized organizational performance results. As a result, public companies have started to reexamine how they are structuring the pay of their

CEOs in order to be in greater congruence to the company performance and value to interested shareholders.

Others have argued that CEO performance in relation to organizational performance is actually quite fair and appears to be on the decline in relation to the performance of their companies. Echoing this view is DeCarlo (2010), who indicated that:

> For the third consecutive year, the chief executives of the 500 biggest companies in the U.S. (as measured by a composite ranking of sales, profits, assets and market value) took a reduction in total compensation. The latest collective pay cut, 30%, was the biggest of the past three years (11% and 15% declines in the prior two years). This marks the first time in the past 20 years that total compensation declined in three consecutive years. In total, these 500 executives earned $4 billion in 2009, which averages out to $8 million apiece. Although down from last year (49%), the value realized from exercised stock options again account for the main component of pay, 30%, this year. The average stock gain was $2.4 million, the lowest since 2004. (p. 1)

Kaplan and Rauh (2008) also concluded that the high level of compensation of CEOs was on par with other top income earners in other industries. The researchers' findings led them to believe that the four sectors composed of high-income earners included top executives, financial service sector employees, corporate lawyers, and professional athletes and celebrities. The researchers proposed that the high level of compensation was a side effect of existing in an elevated earning curve of society. If a person was in one of these populations, it was not considered to be inequality of pay, but rather a natural byproduct within those market populations. Justifying CEO pay in an alternative way was suggested by Gabaix and Landier (2008), noting that the increase in market capitalization was correlated with the increase in CEO pay from 1980 to 2003. They presented a model that predicatively adjusted CEO compensation to the market increasing over the same period of time.

Many companies have used salary incentive-based models in the past to justify increased CEO payments for organizational results. Albeit, there has not been any conclusive evidence to prove that these two variables are directly related to one another (Miller, D., 1995) with CEO compensation rising sharply in the early 1990s. The total compensation for S & P 500 CEOs, involving salary, comprehensive bonuses, stock options, and all other reimbursement, climbed from $2.3 million in 1992 to over $6.5 million in 2000, while stock options increased from 27% to 51% of the total compensation package. In addition, pay in small companies grew from $823,000 to $1.8 million, as pay in medium companies grew from $1.4 million to $3.2 million (Murphy, 2002). The idea that compensation can be directly connected with individual performance appears to be interwoven into compensation theoretical underpinnings. Lo (2006) noted that a compensation package that is well-planned can provide the proper incentives for successful managers to advance company performance.

CEO-Related Compensation Legislation

The Revenue Reconciliation
Act of 1993
One of the first legislative acts that was passed in the early 1990s by the U.S. Congress in an effort to standardize CEO compensation was the Revenue Reconciliation Act of 1993. Supporting evidence appeared in Attaway (1999), who noted that:

This new tax law is applicable to any payment that would be deductible in a tax year beginning after December 31, 1993. Two major exceptions to the $1 million limitation are compensation paid on a commission basis and qualified performance based compensation. In general, compensation must meet the following four requirements to be considered performance based: (1) it must be paid solely on account of the attainment of one or more preestablished objective goals; (2) the performance goal(s) must be established by a compensation committee comprised solely to two or more outside directors; (3) the material terms of the performance goal(s) must be disclosed to and subsequently approved by the shareholders; and (4) the compensation committee must certify that the performance goals have, in fact been satisfied. (p. 104)

The Revenue Reconciliation Act of 1993 was intended to generate value creation for CEO performance by associating it closer to organizational achievements for any amount that was greater than $1 million. However, the CEOs of many companies were already earning less than the $1 million mark, so when the companies increased their CEO revenue to fit this model, it gave the appearance of impropriety in many of them (Brown & Meade, 1997). Much of the legislation that was related to CEO compensation seemed to have been enacted to govern larger sized companies, and in the effort to do so there was no accounting for the negative effects that would impact the much smaller companies.

The Sarbanes-Oxley Act
of 2002

According to Leonard and Salvatore (2002), the Sarbanes-Oxley Act of 2002 (SOX) was a federal law that was put into place by President George Bush for public companies and accounting firms and did not apply to most private companies. In large part, the law was enacted as a response to the public outrage of the recent ethical and financial scandals involving certain public organizations. The SOX Act gives workforce members government protection for reporting claims of firm misbehavior. Furthermore, it provides possible prosecution against public companies for discriminating against workers, who choose to inform regarding illegal firm activities.

The SOX Act was introduced and supported by both U.S. Senator Paul Sarbanes (D-MD) who had served five terms in the Senate, three terms in the House of Representatives, and was a Rhodes Scholar, and *U.S.* Representative Michael G. Oxley (R-OH) who had retired after 25 years of service to Congress, was an ex-FBI agent, who later became the Vice Chairman of Nasdaq. Interestingly, the two men were considered to be sharply contrasted by the very nature of their personalities. Oxley expressed that in the spring of 2002, he and the House Financials Service Committee had worked to create a law that would repair the public's belief in the economic market after the scandals of Enron and other organizations (Farrell, 2007).

There were diverse perspectives on the viability of this law and considerable evidence to support the many opinions that have been widely debated and discussed. So far there have been 88 companies that have been held legally responsible for violations of the law. The Organization for Economic Cooperation and Development supported and endorsed the law, giving it enthusiastic approval for the new standards and approved the whistleblower provisions that were also included in the legislation *(Wall Street Journal*, 2010).

Finally, the effects of the SOX Act have had other repercussions that are not always obvious to the average worker. One of the most critically distinguishing factors in the Act is that upper level executives and 10% of shareholders must file SEC information by the end of the 2nd day of conducting their business affairs. This requirement pertains to stock options for executive officers, which formerly could be released in the first 45 days of the fiscal year. Section 402 of the Act also prohibited any loans to be given to upper level management (Bill Summary, 2009).

One of the biggest points of contention in this legislation was the difference between the effects on small and large sized companies. This lack of equality has led some proponents of the bill to question their judgment of its fairness between greater and lesser revenue-producing firms. In addition, there have been several studies that have shown that many of the undersized corporations, both foreign and domestic, have financial motivations from the deregistration that has occurred in the U.S. stock exchanges (Hurt, 2003). It appears that this may hinder the USA's strength in competing with foreign markets and further limits the resources available to the financial sector.

There were many financial experts who believed that "The Say on Pay Bill" was a reaction to agency theory as recognized by Karni (2007):

The analysis of the principal-agent relationship in the presence of moral hazard often invokes the parameterized distribution formulation. Pioneered and popularized by Mirrlees (1974, 1976), this formulation relies on the existence, at the primitive level, of a family of distribution functions on a set of outcomes, parameterized by the agent's actions. 1. Despite its widespread use, the axiomatic underpinnings of the conducts of the principal and the agent in this theory have not been explored. This paper fills this gap. As usual, the study of the axiomatic foundations is intended to uncover the assumptions implicit in the specification of the objective functions of the parties involved. The understanding of these assumptions helps evaluate the plausibility of the model and provides insight into its behavioral underpinning. (pp. 337338)

Furthermore, according to Shen et al. (2010), the executive compensation package included a principal-agent relationship in which the organization affirms to provide certain incentives in return for the CEO's management of the company. The executive is provided the firm assets, which may create conflicts attributed to agency theory or the principal-agent relationship. The price of ensuring the CEO, who is considered the *agent*, and guaranteeing that the firm resources are properly used for the *stakeholders'* wellbeing while reducing the self-centered interests of the CEO or agent are recognized as the agency conflicts or costs. The concept encompasses one of the current and major conflicts in CEO compensation and firm performance.

Bebchuk and Fried (2004) highlighted many of the perspectives as they are related to the public in general. They pointed to the dilemma in straightforward terms, summarizing the principal-agent model and were critical of the traditional scheme in which CEOs agree with idea incentives that motivate them to provide stockholders with the paramount outcomes, which are based upon traditional principal-agent modeling. Bebchuk and Fried argued that executives, who have more influence on board members, also have more say about their pay than has been accounted for in many of the compensation plans. The researchers acknowledged that changing policy and portraying executive compensation systems with CEOs considered as taking rent from their firms was an option, as opposed to a perfectly incentive-based motivational system. However, Weisbach (2007) expressed doubt as to how effective these modifications could be in executive compensation reformation.

Longnecker, Crawford, and Henke (2010) asserted that in connection with this type of situation, the "Say on Pay Bill" provided shareholders with the chance to vote on executive compensation in a simple "yes" or "no" manner. The choice was only provided for the top five executives in a public company, and the law did not apply to companies that make less than $75 million in market capitalization or less than $50 million in annual revenue.

S. Miller (2010) believed that the Say on Pay Bill could also have been predisposed to proxy advisor's authority because a Tower Watson survey found that 59% of the participants thought that surrogate consulting companies were involved in executive compensation packages, 44% of the firms admitted engaging with proxy advisors over significant areas, 29% confirmed meeting important stakeholders, and only 23% had prescribed an official communication agenda. This information forewarned that there might be a change in scrutiny in the power dynamics because of the effect of the bill.

In recent years, there have been several public companies that have adopted shareholder votes related to executive compensation; however, any firms that received federal assistance through the Troubled Asset Relief Program (TARP) are not included among this group. Three companies, including Motorola, Occidental, and KeyCorp, have had investors decline compensation that was offered to executives (Longnecker et al., 2010). Furthermore, the bill warranted the Securities and Exchange Commission (SEC) to exclude select organizations from the bill and also called for the potential influence of its force to be related to smaller companies. Finally, it dictated that the Federal Government Accountability Office link models of compensation with financial risk taking (Bill Summary, 2009).

In conclusion, many of the different perspectives on how to balance the relationship between the executive and the shareholders were evident from the previously mentioned points of view as well as the inherent challenges that have been experienced in accounting for the possible changes that have occurred. The next section addresses the issues of the CEO compensation packages.

CEO Compensation Packages

The main component of the total CEO compensation packages appeared to be stock options, although many other elements that were included as part of the CEO's tenure have always been closely aligned with the performance of their stocks since the 1970s (Kaplan, 2008). Kaplan noted that there were three main issues that should be considered regarding this issue, including (a) the last 15 years had been successful for the U.S. economy in correlation with the time that CEO compensation had been under harsh scrutiny; (b) the CEO's compensation had shown equality in ratio to other industry's salary increases, pointing to the agency challenge in the U.S. economic system; and (c) higher CEO compensation was connected to better returns in the organization.

Components of CEO Compensation
and Firm Performance

Ellig (1982) recognized five basic components of the CEO compensation, including (a) the remuneration that the CEO received, and frequently this took into consideration examining continuous performance; (b) the benefits for the worker, including health care, retirement coverage, and other related items; (c) usually short-term incentives that were intended as rewards for an annual target; (d) long-term incentives that were typically calculated over several years; and (e) executives had access to perquisites that were benefits intended only for them to the exclusion of other employees. Base pay might also be included in combination with variable pay, which usually incorporated short-term incentives.

According to Wiseman and Gomez-Mejia (1998), there was a distinction between base salary and variable pay among the executives; however, if there was a strong reliance on variable pay instead of base salary, the two reimbursement packages could become indistinguishable. It was important to note that the choices the executives made depended more heavily upon the risks they seemed willing to take.

The CEO compensation SEC categorization system was recently reclassified and is defined as:

1. Salary: The CEO name and association is received directly from the SEC filing proxy statement. There are no CEO alterations in the website after the fiscal year, with salary being defined as paid to the CEO in that financial year.
2. Bonus: CEO bonus is considered paid in the period of that monetary year.
3. Value of Stock and Option Awards: The value combinations of both are cataloged in the summary compensation table, with stock options allowing a CEO to acquire a certain amount of common stock at a confirmed price for a precise amount of time, contrasted to stock awards that are structured in stock that could be classified in time or performance testing.
4. Nonequity Incentive Plan Compensation: These are all other plans specified as equity or stock and, in general, these plans are designed to provide additional motivation for performance enhancement during a period of time.
5. Change in Pension Value and Nonqualified Deferred Compensation Earnings: The definition of this is determined by the actuarial assessment that has been assigned to employee turnover, pension plans, and wages on nonqualified deferred plans during the prior year.
6. All Other Compensation: The classification includes all other perks and benefits received by the CEO, which may include limousines, personal airplanes, golf club memberships, expense accounts, reimbursements, or insurance arrangements. The fees paid to savings plans are part of the

adjustment in pension value and nonqualified deferred compensation earnings.

7. Total Compensation: This is calculated by totaling all the other components, including the salary, bonus, all other compensation, value of stock and option awards, value of nonequity incentive plan compensation, and change in pension values and nonqualified deferred compensation earnings (American Federation of Labor, 2011).

Firm Performance Measurements

Firm performance can be measured in many ways by a variety of different financial ratios. For example, the liquidity ratios measure the quality and adequacy of current assets to meet current obligations as they come due. In other words, "can a firm quickly convert its assets to cash-without a loss--in order to meet its immediate and short-term obligations?" (The Risk Management Association, 20052006, p. 13). The profitability ratios are defined as an organization's capacity to produce revenues and the general financial performance of the company. Profitability ratios have been defined as earnings per share and return on equity (Boone & Kurtz, 2006), and revenue has been defined as the income of the firm from their most recent annual financial information (SEC EDGAR website, 2010a). The earnings per share is the cash value existing to allocate to each share (SEC EDGAR website, 2010b) and the formula for this is indicated as: (EPS) = Net Income - Dividends on Preferred Stock/Common Shares Outstanding (Shim, Siegel, & Simon, 2004).

An important aspect of EPS that is often ignored is the capital, that which is required to generate the earnings (net income) in the calculation. Two companies could generate the same EPS number, but one could do so with less equity (investment) and that company would be more efficient at using its capital to generate income, and by comparison one would be a more successful and effective company (Investopedia.com, 2010). The pretax return on equity (PreTax ROE) is the price of return on the investment by the shareholders and is defined as pretax earning before tax divided by total equity (Pretax earnings before tax/total equity; SEC EDGAR website, 2010c).

Leverage, Solvency, and Debt Ratios

Debt and solvency ratios can measure a firm's ability to pay its interest payments and long-term responsibilities (Pitts, 2006). Leverage ratios can also assess the degree to which a company requires debt to fund its businesses. The debt an organization possesses can definitely influence the firm's capacity to reimburse finances in future dealings. Overall, the investors may prefer to deal with firms that have self-sufficient funds for investment. The leverage ratio has been defined as debt-to-equity ratio (Boone & Kurtz, 2006), and the percentage of principal supplied by creditors opposed to shareholders is seen as total debt/total equity (SEC EDGAR website, 2010c).

According to Filatotchev and Allcock (2010), a contingency approach to CEO compensation can be more advantageous for companies depending on their industry, country, and firm circumstances. The researchers asserted that many of the current compensation packages centered on the general assumption that there was a direct relationship between rewards and performance results. This was largely connected to the idea of the principal-agent structure. Moreover, they believed that there was a difference in the policy between the definitions of *hard law* and *soft law* and examined the unaccounted practices of compensation in the corporate environment.

Jensen and Murphy (1990) noted that these conceptual structures had implications believing that "Agency theory predicts that compensation policy will tie the agent's expected utility to the principal's objective. The objective of shareholders is to maximize wealth; therefore agency theory predicts that CEO compensation policies will depend on changes in shareholder wealth" (pp. 242-243). This suggested that there were other elements that may also have been unaccounted for as this was regarded as a *closed system* approach, confined in many respects by the general cultural context that have limited exclusive contexts attached to their organizations. Although there have been many studies that have shown that one system has not been proven to fit all compensation packages, there are a number of organizations that have adopted the best practices, which has been effective for a number of organizations. Additionally, suggestions have been made to include more specific compensation packages in adherence to businesses' internal and external resources, understanding the stages of the organizational life cycle, assessing the diversity of the management team, and aligning corporate governance practices with similar institutions.

Jensen (1986) suggested that much of the research has been based on the principal-agency model and that by utilizing certain corporate controls, companies could more easily maximize operations. Filatotchev and Allcock

(2010) noted that the major principal-agency dilemma was that the shareholders as *principals* had particularly different interests than the managers as *agents*, and hence could increase the participation in self-interested conduct on the part of a manager or executive. In many cases, this has led to the increased focus on executive compensation monetary incentives in an effort to bring alignment between the interests of both parties.

The normative principal-agent perspective vs. contingency framework of executive compensation highlights and attempts to take into account the constructs that have not been typically incorporated into the principal-agent model and endeavored to illustrate that straightforward incentives are not always necessarily associated with direct organizational results by taking into account a greater number of organizational variables that have traditionally been ignored by the more fast-paced firms. Although the firm participants are the same between the two models in terms of managers and shareholders, the contingency framework specifically accounts for the stakeholders and what they add to the value of the equation that has been created for traditional executive compensation packages (Filatotchev & Allcock, 2010).

The Organizational and Corporate Governance Dynamics concept distinguishes between the distinct life phases of each company. For example, Quadrant 1 illustrates the start-up, small firms, and institutional development projects, while Quadrant 2 exhibits organizations on the brink or in the process of initial public offering (IPOs). Quadrant 3 addresses the established companies, and finally, Quadrant 4 includes the companies on the decline or on the verge of a public takeover (Filatotchev & Allcock, 2010). The authors noted that the contingency structure of the organization should be interwoven with the life cycle and stages of growth that are occurring. The dynamics of age, size, developmental stage, and internal or external forces all appear to contribute to the corporate governance of the organization. Filatotchev and Bishop (2002) also believed that the organizational life cycle (OLC) was essential to the executive compensation package that was instituted in each firm. The incentives and rewards should be aligned with the particular OLC stage of the organization. For example, more established companies may be concerned with lessening agency costs by reward arrangement in comparison to start-up firms, which are looking at the challenges of managers predicting technological growth and less concerned with executive level compensation alignment.

The executive compensation packages may also be affected by the national institution's location. Most of the research has been focused on studying the outcomes of executive incentive components in the United States and the United Kingdom (U.K.) in the corporate sector. Yet, many of the components in these executive pay packages certainly do not apply to other countries.

Filatotchev and Allcock (2010) provided evidence of the variations in compensation packages among countries by presenting a structural percentage breakdown of CEO compensation in the largest companies in countries other than the U.S. or U.K. For example, the base salary in the U.S. is only 23%, cash bonus is 17%, and incentive plan is 60%. This is in contrast to Ireland where the base salary is 44%, cash bonus is 43%, and incentive plan is 13%, and to Japan where base salary is 71%, cash bonus is 12%, and incentive plan is 17%. It should be noted that these companies are only included from revenues of $1 billion to $3 billion.

These differences vary across other countries and have implications of widespread discrepancies related to the contingency models. The possibility exists that some of the national institutions may also have similarities across some countries (Filatotchev & Allcock, 2010). Additionally, Weisbach (2007) noted that distinct governance compositions occurred from diverse financial institutional procedures. The executive compensation compositions differed across the globe from Europe, Japan, and the USA. Because of the uniqueness of the economics in each country, it may well be challenging to justify the optimal balance.

In summary, this section has examined the background and history of CEO compensation, the Revenue Reconciliation Act of 1993, Sarbanes-Oxley Act of 2002, Say on Pay Bill, total compensation packages, and elements of compensation, which have been explored and discussed as being some of the most powerful influences that are related to compensation issues. It has demonstrated that there has been a propensity to understand and fairly distribute executive compensation; however, the attempts to account for its accountability and control have indicated that in many respects it appears to be out of balance with the desires of the population at large.

While this chapter examined CEO compensation in great detail and explored the relationship to organizational performance, the next chapter describes the methodology for examining the CEO compensation in relationship to the U.S.-based public global insurance firms' organizational performance. The sources for accessing the data are presented, along with the methods that were used to examine the compensation packages.

3
Methodology

Purpose

The purpose of this research project was to determine the strength of the connection or relationship between a CEO's compensation and the performance of the firm in the public, global insurance domain. The *Forbes Magazine's Global 2000 List* was utilized as the basis for the examination, with the researcher making a selection of the top 20 USA public, globally based insurance companies. These companies and their related data were examined for the years 2007, 2008, and 2009, utilizing the Statistical Package for Social Sciences (SPSS).

The context of this project was the examination of compensation for chief executive officers (CEOs) and the possible correlation with organizational performance in multinational, public insurance companies. The research was focused on the reimbursement components (salaries and incentives) of the CEOs as they translated to organizational performance in their particular companies. Organizational performance was defined by earnings per share (EPS), debt-to-equity, revenue, and pretaxed return on equity (ROE). The elements of organizational performance were compared with the components of CEO compensation, which consisted of salary, stock awards, option awards, other compensation, nonequity compensation, deferred compensation, and total compensation, as well as the acknowledged rankings of the insurance companies within these domains. The organizational and compensation variables for the CEOs were found in the 10k and DEF14A, or SEC proxy filings for each organization that was chosen.

The analysis of the data was performed across 3 years (2007-2009) or in a parallel comparison, and an examination of the prior year's performance relative to the subsequent year's CEO compensation was utilized to discover the relationship between predictive strategies. A backward multiple regression analysis was employed due to the ordinal data available, and an assessment was performed for all three of the hypotheses for the years 2007, 2008, and 2009. The figures were extracted from public sources of consolidated information and consisted of data from the SEC filings for the years 2007, 2008, and 2009. The evaluation was conducted at a significance correlation alpha level of .05.

The research questions were organized into different subhypotheses related to several factors and the relationships to organizational performance. These factors included the global insurance firms based in the USA, financial analysis of the companies, and detailed incentive packages for their CEOs. This methodology utilized a quasi-test research design focused on the use of the available public and archival data for the insurance industry. The study examined the relationship of several critical variables in order to draw conclusions about the correlation of organizational performance with CEO reimbursement.

Hypotheses

There were three hypotheses being tested using statistical correlations, percentiles, or both to determine if (a) Hypothesis 1: There is a significant relationship between CEO total compensation and firm performance, (b) Hypothesis 2--There is a significant relationship between CEO base salary and company performance, and (c) Hypothesis 3--There is a significant relationship between previous year's organizational performance and CEO compensation.

In summary, the methodology was focused on utilizing public, archival data that were readily available through several databases and other related resources. Organizational performance was compared with CEO compensation in the *Forbes Magazine's* top 20, global, public insurance companies for the years 2007, 2008, and 2009. Since all of the data that were retrieved for these research questions were extracted from public sources that were readily available and easily searched, there was little or no risk of harm to the individual CEOs who were chosen for the study, and the process did not involve any procedures for which written consent would normally have been required. There was also no need of storing the data in a secured location or appropriately disposing of it when the study was completed since any individual could have also accessed the data on his or her own.

This chapter was an explanation of the methodology of the examination of the hypotheses of CEO total compensation and firm performance, CEO base salary and firm performance, and overall CEO compensation and firm performance from a lagged year measurement. The next chapter contains the

results of the assessment of the relationship between CEO compensation and
U.S.-based public, global insurance organizations' performance.

4
Results

The purpose of this research project was to determine the strength of the association between CEOs' compensation and the performance of their firms in the insurance industry. The *Forbes Magazine's Global 2000* List was used as the basis of this project, and the researcher selected the top 20 USA, public-based insurance companies. These companies had both compiled data and evaluated data for the years 2007, 2008, and 2009, and the Statistical Package for social Sciences (SPSS) was utilized for evaluation of the data.

In exploration of this objective for each of the multiple components of CEO compensation and total CEO compensation, regression was performed on the primary indicators of financial performance for the 20 insurance companies. A backward elimination strategy was employed in order to maximize the probability of identifying one or more significant predictors. Since it could not be established when the various CEO pay components were specified (i.e., at the beginning of a year on the basis of a previous year's performance or at the end of a year on the basis of a current year's performance), the analyses were performed on both the nonlagged and lagged basis. The nonlagged analyses used the CEO compensation levels and the firm performance measures for the same years. This analysis used 3 years of data for each firm, while the lagged analyses used the CEO compensation levels for 2008 and 2009 and firm performance data for 2007 and 2008, respectively. The lagged analyses had 1/3 fewer observations than did the nonlagged analyses due to the effect of the lagging.

The variables that were used included firm performance measured by earnings per share, debt-to-equity ratio, revenue, and pretax return on earnings (ROE). The CEO compensation variables were measured in terms of base salary, stock awards, stock options, other compensation, nonequity incentives, deferred compensation, and total compensation. A backward multiple regression analysis was employed due to the ordinal data available. An evaluation was performed for all three hypotheses for the years 2007, 2008, and 2009. The components of CEO compensation and the measures of firm performance that were used in this study are reported in Tables 1 and 2.

Table 1

*Components of CEO Compensation and
Measures of Firm Performance*

CEO compensation component	Firm performance measure
Salary	Earnings per share
Stock awards	Debt-to-equity ratio
Stock options	Revenue
Other compensation	Pretax return on earnings (ROE)
Nonequity incentives	
Deferred compensation	
Total compensation	

Table 2

Results of Regressions of CEO Compensation Components on Concurrent Measures of Performance of Insurance Firms During 2007-2009

CEO Compensation component	Significant firm performance predictors	b	SEb	β	t	p	Adjusted R²
	(Constant)	1,045,944.43	47052.86		22.23	< .001	
Salary							.169
	Earnings per share	1,331.38	417.55	.43	3.19	.003	
Stock awards	None						
Stock options	None						
Other compensation	None						
Nonequity incentives	None						
Deferred compensation	None						
	Constant	11,088,352.44	884,031.70		11.73	.000	
Total compensation							.096
	Pretax ROE	61,825.80	25,472.38	.34	2.43	.019	

Hypotheses Testing

Results for
Hypothesis 1

The first hypothesis predicted that there would be a significant relationship between CEO total compensation and firm performance. Table 1 also indicates a coefficient of determination (r-squared) of .096 *(p* = .019) between CEO total compensation and pretax return on equity (firm performance), indicating that the strength of the relationship was significant and within the top 20 companies ranked on the results of the regressions of CEO compensation components on concurrent measures of performance of insurance firms during 2007, 2008, and 2009.

Results for
Hypothesis 2

The second hypothesis predicted that there would be a significant relationship between CEO base salary and firm performance. Table 2 shows a coefficient of determination (r-squared) of .169 *(p* = .003) between CEO base salary and earnings per share (firm performance), indicating that this was a significant firm predictor of CEO compensation and within the top 20 companies ranked on the results of regressions of CEO compensation components on concurrent measures of performance of insurance firms during 2007, 2008, and 2009. The results for each of the concurrent analyses are reported in Table 2.

Results for
Hypothesis 3

The third hypothesis predicted that there would be significant relationships between the prior year's organizational performance and CEO compensation. In this case, Table 3 shows the results of regressions of CEO compensation components using lagged measures of performance of the insurance firms during 2008-2009. This process compared firm performance from the previous year(s) and compared it with CEO compensation for the following year(s). In this analysis, there were stronger predictive relationships determined between firm performance and CEO compensation. Table 3 indicated a coefficient of determination (r-squared) of .128 *(p* = .023) between CEO base salary and revenue (firm performance). There was a significant relationship between CEO other compensation and revenue with a coefficient of determination (r-squared) of .182 *(p* = .012). Finally, a predictive relationship was found linking CEO deferred compensation and revenue, demonstrated by a coefficient of determination (r-squared) of .206 *(p* = .008). The results for each of the lagged analyses are reported in Table 3.

Summary

This chapter described the results of the hypotheses of CEO total compensation and firm performance, CEO base salary and firm performance, and overall CEO compensation and firm performance from a lagged year measurement. The next chapter presents a discussion of the implications of the results, as well as proposals for understanding CEO compensation and firm performance. The chapter also discusses areas of possible future research that focuses on executive compensation and organizational performance.

Table 3

Results of Regressions of CEO Compensation Components on Lagged Measures of Performance of Insurance Firms During 2008-2009

CEO Compensation component	Significant firm performance predictors	b	SEb	o	t	ID	Adjusted 122
Salary	(Constant)	1,164,279.40	84,918.95		13.71	.000	
	Revenue	-.00	.00	-.40	-2.39	.023	.128
Stock awards	None						
Stock options	None						
Other compensation	(Constant)	812,283.93	665,558.86		1.22	.233	
	Revenue	.00	.00	.46	2.69	.012	.182
Nonequity incentives	None						
Deferred compensation	(Constant)	17,398.94	720,989.26		.02	.981	
	Revenue	.00	.00	.48	2.88	.008	.206
Total compensation	None						.096

5
Discussion

This chapter is divided into three sections, with the first one featuring an overview of the findings of the results, reflecting on the implications as they relate to the information regarding CEO compensation. The limitations of this study are also presented for providing a greater understanding of the examination of the compensation models. Finally, recommendations for possible future research are discussed, along with the application to the field of organization development.

The purpose of this project was to gain a greater understanding between the relationship of CEO compensation and organizational performance in U.S.-based, multinational insurance companies. The *Forbes Magazine's Global 2000 List* was comprised of 20 insurance companies for the year 2009. These companies were then examined for a 3-year period that encompassed the years 2007, 2008, and 2009 to determine if there were any predictive relationships between the CEO compensation variables and organizational performance variables. A reverse method of multiple regression omission was conducted on each of the CEO compensation components to identify the firm performance indices that were useful predictors. Each firm variable was isolated, compared, and removed to determine relationships with CEO variables and any correlations that might exist among variables. The companies consisted of a variety of USA-based, multinational insurance companies that ranked from 90th to 1148th by the *Forbes Magazine's Global 2000* data sources in the year 2009.

The data were focused on whether there was a significant relationship between CEO total compensation and organizational performance, also exploring if there was a significant relationship between CEO base salary and firm performance. A third inquiry examined if there were significant relationships between the prior year's organizational performance and CEO compensation.

The only two components of CEO compensation that proved to be significantly predictable by concurrent measures of firm performance were salary and total compensation. Although the prediction of these aspects of compensation reached statistically significant levels, the effect sizes were quite modest: 16.9% of the variance in the case of salary and 9.6% of the variance in the case of total compensation.

The results for the lagged firm performance measures discovered that the lagged measures were more predictive of aspects of CEO compensation in these firms than the simultaneous measures. Specifically, revenue level in the prior year significantly predicted CEO base salary, other compensation, and deferred compensation.

Limitations

The analysis of the data for this research project was limited to SEC filings from companies on a nonsequential manner and CEO compensation filed at various times. The total compensation components were researched, and there was miscellaneous data unification. The components of salary, bonuses, restricted stock awards, all other compensation, option awards, nonequity incentive plan compensation, change in pension value, nonqualified deferred compensation earnings, and total compensation varied with the reporting of firms. The sample of the corporations that was taken from the *Forbes Magazine's Global 2000* was limited to the top 20 multinational insurance companies that were all based in the United States.

The data were also limited by the firm performances in certain organizations because of the SEC sanctions. These firms may have been better served measuring the median in certain financial sectors. The performance of such companies tends to skew the overall structure of the analysis and inflates or deflates some performances. The sample size of $N =$ 20 was rather small and limited. In general, pure bonuses were virtually absent within the definitions of the component packages and appeared to have evolved into other forms of incentives. Some of the firms were not present in each of the years 2007, 2008, and 2009; therefore, the most effective method of finding predictors was to group them together for a comparison, which encompassed an across company, 3-year data analysis starting from the year 2009 and then subsequently perform a secondary lagged analysis from 1 year to another. The second analysis performed provided a more in-depth predictor of the company performances than did the first analysis.

Implications

The focus of this study examined the strength of the relationship between firm variables and aspects of CEO compensation within the *Forbes Magazine's Global 2000* top 20, U.S.-based, multinational insurance organizations. Consistently tracking the various firms in an assortment of settings may prove to be more conducive to the improvement of the process, and studying CEO compensation in situational framework could be far more inclusive than just pure assessment of relational numbers.

Recommendations

The first recommendation would be to involve the contextuality of the company with the compensation and CEO incentives. According to Filatotchev and Allcock (2010), accounting for the background framework that is unique and specific to company situation would be more important to performance rather than routine connections of rewards and executive compensation. In addition, Porter and Siggelow (2008) suggested that within an organization, interactions also may have a strong influence on the sustainability and success in many firms. This two-pronged approach could prove to be far more effective for companies that are trying to maintain viability and increase effectiveness within their industries. Traditionally, this approach has not been given much precedence in organizations for a variety of reasons; however, for future research it may represent a more competitive advantage.

The second recommendation would be to review unused alternative options, such as having life insurance, as a competitive edge in the benefits of CEO compensation. Examples were acknowledged and discussed in Bell and Pickart's (2007) work through taxable bonuses, premium payments, policy distributions, and loss benefits.

The third recommendation examines various options from a range of programs such as child care, extended maternity/paternity programs (Jordan-Evans & Kaye, 2005), and stock options--all of which can be used to supplement the incentives for executive compensation, but seldom have been explored by the firms. Finally, according to Hall (2001), aligning stock option plans with the situational needs of the firm could be invaluable to management of alignment of CEO compensation. The concepts of fixed value plans, fixed number plans, or megagrant plans are methods that are adjustable to unique circumstances. The key would be to appropriately match the qualified requirements of the company with the proper stock option plans available. Porter and Siggelow (2008) referred to the sustainability and longevity of a firm in terms of theoretical research of firm profitability related to interactional approaches in activity to enhance the processes of relationship management.

Context

One implication of this research project for the field of organization development (OD) is that there should be a more in-depth analysis of the many factors within an organization that are not specifically related to compensation. While compensation needs to be connected to companies' performance, understanding the context and culture within those firms may be equally important to the outcomes and need more integration. Cummings and Worley (2005) advocated a multiple level OD plan that included various analyses, including history, action theories, global considerations, cross-cultural studies, and joint ventures between scholars and practitioners who could bring different perspectives to the table.

This project examined CEO compensation in USA-based, global insurance companies over a 3-year period; however, there were many additional factors within the review of the literature that were equally influential and could be examined further for a greater understanding of the issue. For example, a future study of organizational size and prior performance within the insurance field might be of interest. Tosi, Werner, Katz, and Gomez-Mejia (2000) provided evidence that previous company performance and institutional size influenced CEOs' compensation in current organizational performance. The methodology focused on a computation of a firm's employee size, and previous performance was measured by the return on assets (ROA) for the past year period.

Application to the Field of Organization Development

Researching the role the actuaries could bring to OD could allow for greater congruence between the estimation of the categorical numbers and the considerations of the field. Often referred to as informatics, this additional level of available research could be invaluable when evaluating trends, outcomes, and related issues.

One of the most important implications of the study was examining the definitions of the various legislative rulings. The classification of pension value and nonqualified deferred compensation earnings in 2011 was redefined, and greater attention was placed on the change in pension value and nonqualified deferred compensation earnings in terms of the actuarial value to the executive officer. This is the increase in actuarial assessment to the executive officer of all defined benefit pension plans and earnings on nonqualified deferred compensation plans over the past year (American Federation of Labor, 2011). So, in the new era of regulation, the actuaries' interpretation may make an even more significant difference in how they judge CEO compensation variables than it already does. In addition, Shim and Siegel (2008) noted that the *Actuarial Cost (Funding) Method* is a technique for calculating employer contributions to approximate the correct amount of financial support for the employee's retirement. The process is used to make a fairly accurate prediction as to pension expenses and other liabilities. In line with these techniques are a host of other methods an actuary uses, ranging from projected benefit obligation to net assets available for pension benefits, which could provide differential financial analyses for assessing CEO compensation.

From the researcher's perspective, it might be interesting to study if the same information was given to a number of separate actuaries, the rate of commonality of their conclusions. In other words, do different actuaries come to different or identical conclusions with the same available information? If the conclusions are distinctive, then this might point to subjectivity in the procedure, and if there are variations it might prove advantageous to consider process-oriented work. Using an action research methodology could be of particular interest in understanding a U.S.-based, multinational insurance industry.

For example, in this particular situation, the actuaries are in charge of a tremendous amount of business. They can significantly sway the financial rates for their own organization, a number of other firms across the globe, and perhaps even the CEO's company performance results. Therefore, if there was a significant level of a lack of awareness involved in decision making, it could lead to dissimilar assessments on compensation.

Austin and Bartunek (2006) pointed out that action research focuses on the incongruity between people's action and their espoused theories. The focus of Argyris's (2006) research was on double-loop learning that centered on increasing the awareness of the underlying actual values guiding actions and the mental schemas that were influencing their situation. In a group setting, with individuals of different perspectives, a process-driven approach could uncover gaps in judgment, which may perhaps improve efficiency in decision making among the actuaries. A scenario where a group could be composed of key decision makers involved in creating the financial rates would prove to be an optimal situation. In fact, it could be used to construct a clearer understanding of the desired organizational goals.

Thus, if someone is operating as one of the top 20 globally based firms and the desire is to move up in ranking or simply move ahead of the competition, then it might be worth determining the definition of improving processes. Generating a clearer understanding of a company goals in a multinational firm would be essential if it is operating in a global marketplace. For example, if one is in a U.S.-based insurance company and the revenue of the corporation is primarily coming from Japan, it would be important to know if that affects the company's general philosophy of using resources in the USA. If it is a firm and the objective is to increase the EPS for shareholders in the USA but most of the sales are coming from Europe, then there may be a competing objective from that portion of the organization. Finally, if a company espouses *family values*, one question that might be asked is, "Do those values look the same in the U.S. as they do in another nation?" Process-oriented work with key executives can assist in the construction and connection of clarified goals. Adler (2002) noted that "Leaders help to shape the organization's vision, the meaning within which others work and live. Managers, by contrast, act competently within a vision" (p. 165).

In conclusion, a glimpse at the actuaries' participation in the process has been explored, and the idea of using action research and the possible positive result that could be accomplished was presented. The next section investigates the results of the research study as it related to the shareholder's perspective.

Shareholder's Perspective

The results from the first and second hypotheses in this research project illustrated how an investor would understand the view from a value standpoint. The outcomes demonstrated that if a top 20 USA insurance *Forbes Global 2000* company was examined for a continuous 3-year period, from 2007 to 2009, there appears to be a strength of relationship in the aspects of firm performance, which included total compensation, base salary (CEO Performance), as compared to pretax return on equity (pre-ROE), earnings per share (firm performance). From the researcher's point of view, if one were to judge a company and invest money based on the merit, then perhaps a quick examination would suggest to moderate that view accordingly to an advantage on pre-ROE or on EPS to the investor in the last 3-year period to the *Forbes Global 2000* top 20 U.S.-based insurance firms list and understand the constraint of the study to those populations. Thus, if an investor wanted to review these results and study a company, he or she may conclude that on a global level the *Forbes* top 20 listed firms in U.S.-based insurance companies over a 3-year period may allocate capital to these firms on the basis of pretax (ROE) and EPS related to the CEO performance and expect a certain value for his or her investment. The significance may be limited to the categories that were previously listed.

In terms of the third hypothesis, consisting of examining the company on the basis of the prior year's organizational performance and CEO compensation, the data suggested that if a stockholder wanted to forecast the CEO's compensation for the following year, he or she could reasonably ascertain that the relationship would be significant between the areas of CEO salary and revenue, CEO other compensation and revenue, and CEO deferred compensation and revenue. In this case, it appears that if a shareholder wanted to forecast whether a CEO would receive greater gratuities the following year, it might reasonably be predicted that it would on the basis of this research project. This project could be used if shareholders wanted to enhance or prevent certain CEO compensation practices related to salary, deferred compensation, and stock options and perhaps make them connect contingent pay to the short-, medium-, or long-term organizational development goals of the firm.

Hall (2001) described some three different stock option plans:

1. Fixed value plans, which are usually a sequence of yearly grants with a consistent value or held in ratio to the executive base salary or total compensation: An instance of this might be when a CEO of one of the insurance companies would be given $2 million for each year for 5 years or a value of two times the CEO's income for the same period of years. This plan is usually applied when a firm is trying to reduce the retention risk. In other words, if a company simply wants to make certain they keep the executive, then this plan is a convenient means of attaining that goal. Because the executive knows that if stock price falls for the company, he or she will still be assured of a hefty grant the following

year, and this allows for having a definite stake in the business. The plan, however, is not usually the most motivational one for creating greater value in the company.

2. Fixed number plan, which is a design of 12-month period grants with a set number of options: An illustration of this would be a CEO who is given $50,000 options--5 years for each year. The important stipulation here is that these options are *at-the-money* worth; therefore, the option that is exercised is equal to the exact stock price it was valued at the time when it was granted. The potency of this plan is that it creates greater motivation for a CEO to create greater value for the firm since at-the-money options are intertwined with the stock prices of the organization. Thus, if the stock declines in price, then so does one of the compensation components. The plan is useful for organizations that are using fixed value plans that desire to provide more enticements to executives in creating greater value for the business. The plan is also applicable to postinitial public offering firms, which are still startups, and are using megagrants.

3. Megagrants are the third option presented by Hall (2001). These grants are straight, at-the-money options in the present year, and nothing is received in the next set number of years. So, a CEO may receive $300,000 the 1st year and zero for the next 5 years. A plan like this usually generates the most motivation for an executive to do his or her best to create value for the firm. Therefore, if the value of that stock drops, the company may not retain the executive very long. One of the ways in which companies try to keep the executives is by changing the price of the original options under these circumstances. These types of plans are usually utilized by large corporations with aspirations for fresh and new leadership who are not concerned about an executive leaving in the event of a devaluation of the stock. The plan is not a match for start-ups that may experience fluctuating prices in the value of their stock and need to create stability among upper management.

In summary, the type of plan that a company adopts to create should greatly depend upon the long-term goals of the firm. The previous three types of grants and option plans were clearly dictated by the needs of the organization. The next section explores coaching and its relationship to the CEOs.

Coaching and CEOs

The results from the first and second hypotheses in this research project illustrated that the outcomes could serve as proof to the effectiveness of one's leadership in the areas of pre-ROE and EPS to the company and its investors. The areas could possibly be used to serve as justification between the CEO base salary and total compensation packages and during a continuous 3-year period (2007 to 2009), and the results would have shown the strength of relationship in those facets of performance. Additionally, the results could also support validation for the CEO arguing hypothetically that he or she should receive greater compensation for the components of base salary, other compensation, and deferred compensation based on revenue production in the prior year. This concept could also be used to negotiate for future compensation based on revenue performance.

The insurance industry is highly competitive and, like many others similar to it, competitors are constantly looking for an edge. One of the ways that a competitive advantage may be accomplished is through the use of coaching for the CEOs and experimenting with 360-degree feedback. Maylett and Riboldi (2007) noted that among the *Fortune 500* firms, almost 90% use some type of 360-degree feedback process and that strong 360-degree feedback scores are correlated with stronger employee engagement, which in turn has been shown in many studies to be related to greater successful financial performance in firms. Some of these economic indicators have been return on investment and increasing stock prices for the companies. These results actually had a lag in their predictability; therefore, a manager who received higher scores on a 360-degree feedback took about 12 to 14 months to show elevated financial performance. Within the realm of 360-degree feedback, Hicks, Peterson, and Uranowitz (1997) noted that with managers from the *Fortune 250*, the most effective feedback that was given to them was described as being clear, constructive, and concise, making it much easier to be able to change behaviors and increase their effectiveness.

From the researcher's experience, the insurance industry could greatly benefit from utilizing feedback processes followed by initiating CEO coaching. Many executives are too busy with *bare boned* financial results to understand how personal behavioral improvement can improve results, nor are they usually rewarded for personal development.

Filipczak (1998) pointed out that CEOs are busier listening to the highlights of the business rather than understanding the smaller details that are being communicated by their employees. Another example that was cited referred to a CEO who was participating in being *shadowed*, a technique whereby the CEO is observed by an executive coach in everyday interactions. In this particular instance, the CEO appeared to do very well in front of the coach, but it was quite different and unmanageable when the CEO was alone with the employees. The dual personalities were described as leaving the employees *gagging*. This situation is more common than not in the researcher's experience from dealing with various executives, especially noting the difference in behavior behind closed doors as compared to behavior in the public eye.

If the lag period results noted in this research project that were specifically related to the predictive quality of revenue results being related to salary, other compensation, and deferred compensation were then coupled with the data of lagged findings (Maylett & Riboldi, 2007), it could possibly provide for a powerful competitive financial performance to a CEO and the organization. Interestingly, an area for future research would be combining these studies with personality styles measured by the Myers Briggs Type Indicator (MBTI) and other competency measurement scales and reviewing the data to see if there were any possible correlation factors that emerged which might lead to higher firm performance.

In summary, an exploration of the applicability of the results of this research project and how they could be related to an executive's position were reviewed. Some of the advantages of 360-degree feedback processes and coaching were presented. The next section explores the relationship between the research project and labor unions.

Labor Unions

The possible consequences from the findings of the first and second hypotheses illustrated that if a labor union wanted to utilize the results for contract negotiations, the effect could serve as validation to the effectiveness of organizational leadership in the areas of pre-ROE and EPS for union workers. However, it could also demonstrate a lack of significant evidence in the company performance measures of debt-to-equity and revenue. A negotiating committee would be in a much better position to consider asking for certain contingencies over a period of time connected to the data that were related to the performance of the CEO, organization, or both.

Although a CEO and the company could explain the executive's base salary and total compensation, the union might request a closer inspection of stock awards, stock options, other compensation, nonequity incentives, and deferred compensation. During a continuous 3-year period (2007-2009), there was a lack of evidence of relationship in those facets of performance. Thus, it could be argued that employee benefits and compensation were related to the executive taking advantage of distinct compensation components that were dependent on company performance variables. In addition, a situation could occur where the organization does produce extra revenue, that it is returned to the workers in the future, and a realignment of the executive compensation package could be done.

Additionally, the labor union could argue that greater compensation for the components of base salary, other compensation, and deferred compensation should be based on revenue production in the prior year and for future years to come. In this case, CEO compensation and firm performance could comparatively be adjusted to any labor concerns based just on the previous year.

In closing, the labor unions have numerous options depending on their perceived needs for the employees. For the purpose of this research project, only the immediate situation has been proposed for the sake of examination. The next section examines the different perspectives of succession planning.

Succession Planning

As the different areas related to the practices of organization development have been examined, they culminate here with exploring the ramifications to succession planning and ultimately to the selection of the top executive in the organization. From a long-term perspective in the company's preparation for future CEOs, succession planning becomes an extremely important issue. If a company wanted to evaluate a potential CEO based on the findings of the first and second hypotheses in this research project, the choice would lend itself to the outcomes that were exemplified from the top 20 USA *Forbes Global 2000* insurance companies that were examined for a continuous 3-year (2007-2009) period, and the company would have chosen a strength of relationship in the aspects of firm performance, which included total compensation, base salary (CEO performance), as weighted against pretax return-on-equity (pre-ROE), earnings per share (firm performance).

In a similar fashion to the first two hypotheses, the information gathered would come from a solitary business, and the executive would have also come from this company. In terms of the third hypothesis, which consisted of examining the company on the basis of the prior year's organizational performance and CEO compensation evidence, choosing a CEO based on the data would mean that the business executive selection was performed according to the significance of relationship between the areas of CEO salary and revenue, CEO other compensation and revenue, and CEO deferred compensation and revenue.

The interesting finding in this kind of assessment is that Hypotheses 1 and 2 would be looking at the research over a concurrent 3-year period and basing the decision on the results in order to choose a new CEO, but in Hypothesis 3, the observation of the data would only be related to the variables from the year before to the year after, and the prior year's company performance factors might be ascribed to the CEO's compensation dynamics in the following year.

Executive selection has increasingly become a hotly debated subject, and the process of selecting a CEO can be a complicated procedure. Hollenback (2009) noted that many people feel that 70% of variance is unaccounted for in relation to executive achievement. Yet, he also argued that performance from prior experiences offers a range of what someone is likely to do in the future. At the same time, he noted that in considerably different circumstances, it can become challenging to predict behavior. Furthering the discussion, the dilemma is that the distinction between selection malfunction versus executive failure may not always be apparent. In other words, understanding which course of action is responsible for the lack of the success of the CEO can be quite complicated to define. Day (2009) noted that executive selection should not be a detached assessment but rather be considered as part of a greater succession management plan. The better quality of the research collection and involvement in the creation of larger literature catalog are also central issues to be taken into account. Charan (2005) noted that the National Association of Corporate Directors found that approximately half the firms generating revenues of better than $500 million did not have a functional succession plan. Moreover, a survey of 276 organizations conducted by The Corporate Leadership Council (CLC) discovered that a mere 20% of the HR executives were content with their top executive succession plans.

In short, there is an urgent need in many companies for a new way of thinking that incorporates succession plans for future leadership to be implemented in a more logical and coherent way. The CEO selection method can prove instrumental in aligning organizational goals with the results of the leadership team. From the researcher's viewpoint, not having a workable succession plan is the equivalent of not having insurance for one's company. The nest section summarizes and highlights some of the important issues that have been presented from the research project.

Summary

The congruence between individual CEO incentive rewards (that are in alignment with personal concerns and values) and organizational contextual alignment (associated with the company's present position in organizational development and societal cultural norms) along with the impact on the ever-present fluctuating global economy is influential on the longer term effects of sustainability. A sample of this evidence came from the *International Insurance Fact Book* (International Insurance Society, 2007-2008) where the document highlighted the simple difference in classification of the insurance industries in and outside of the United States. Within the U.S., the insurance industry was classified as having life and health, property and casualty insurance, while the preponderance of this classification in other countries was called either life, nonlife, or general insurance.

These industries are further comprised of diverse inner insurance categorizations that should be generalized for the purpose of streamlining accounting practices. However, if they were evaluated within an individual type of insurance structure, it would in turn illuminate the variance within the individual firms, highlighting the importance of a contextual framework in sorting the various types of insurance companies.

According to Filatotchev and Allcock (2010), the investigation into the background of the companies in their settings can be extremely beneficial and is related to the issues of CEO compensation. Understanding the conditions of distinct company control systems allows for a more systemic analysis of organizations. The greater the understanding of the uniqueness of the company's exclusive circumstances, the easier it may be to keep track of certain similarities in grouping the blueprints of executive compensation. This type of initiative allows for changing and aligning various styles of organizational contexts, along with various CEO compensation packages. Although the data are often indicative of gains and losses, they cannot predict the totality of the background consequences that hopes to achieve the balanced outcomes which appear to be so enmeshed in controversy at this time.

From the researcher's perspective, more effective accounting should be supplied to the current equations that have been traditionally used to calculate and formulate CEO compensation plots, which have contributed to the present global economic situation, rather than applying the organizational ideas that are consistently endorsed by each company. The enhancement of CEO compensation and firm performance results will not be optimized in the way that they have been achieved in past economic equations that were thought to be more efficient in nature. The new concept consists of combining matured theories with new thought processes that may at times have been considered to be obsolete in the past, yet their usefulness was acknowledged some time ago and is currently being rediscovered in the new workplace.

From an organizational developmental perspective, these forces may be utilized to gain more applied and deeper insight into the maximization of the processes that can be attained by aligning the effects of rewards (intrinsic or extrinsic in nature) that are given to CEO's and the company's performance within the framework of accountability that also incorporates long-term contextual sustainability. This circumstance further requires self-reflection within individuals and organizations in implementing the effectiveness that they purport to be seeking. Whether it consists of a short-term or long-term level, the paramount challenge is to understand the goals of both the individuals and organizations in a collaborative manner. The complexity of combining ideas and then leaving them to be executed from internal mechanisms has often proven to be a fatal flaw in the organization's goals and to the individuals as well. The key to CEO compensation and firm performance is to embrace a greater understanding of the needs and desires of the company, the country, and the larger global community.